I0159053

Copyright ©2022 Farzanah Shah
The Warrior Princess: An Odyssey Through Love

Published by Author using Breeze Publishing's services
www.breezepublishing.co.za
1st Edition 2022 South Africa

Cover by Ushaka Designs
Layout & Design by Ushaka Designs
Printed in

ISBN 978-0-620-98030-2

For my peach
You have impacted my life in the most beautiful way
This one is for you

The Warrior Princess: An Odyssey Through Love

Farzanah Shah

Table Of Contents

Passion

Pain

Power

Passion

Alluring Love

I always said I never knew what love was
Till you came along and showed me the stars
You painted my little world with the colors of youthful passion
And within me a delicate rosebud bloomed in a strange fashion

How was I to know that my little world you would change forever
When you would make me yours and we would finally be together
Strange are the ways of love that fate has brought me to you
Now and forever to keep and treasure, for the sweetest memories
are but few

Take my hand you would say, for I have the world to offer
No, I would say, for I want not the world but your heart of gold
and not copper
I wish to see the world through your love so sweet and pure
That a tender heart like mine it would forever cure

How I wish for you to paint my dreams with the allure of love so
bright
That when my eyes I close, I see only your sweet sight
You quench my thirst for you, like the earth after its first rain
And with your delicate words you caress my soul freeing it from all
pain

This is undoubtedly the allure of love that can never be found
Instead, it demands to be felt, neither with speech nor sound

Bittersweet Love

It's funny how I still think about you
Even if the moments we spent were so few
I tried blocking you out of my mind
Believe me, but it's always your memories I'd find

And I would question myself and sometimes my heart
As to why we were so near yet so far apart
But what answers would I get
For the heart just wouldn't forget

And so, I sit here spilling my thoughts to a piece of paper
Embracing my loneliness, and holding on to a better "later"
But alas, what good is hope, for the heart is already frail
And what good are memories, for they too are gone stale

Letting go is no choice, it's now a must
Neither do I have a wand nor fairy dust
If there is no hope or memories, there is no reason
All there is, is my innocent heart charged with treason

Love is not simple, but it's not math either
Love is painful and beautiful,
That is why I am going to hold onto it,
Or else I will have neither

Passion

First Love

The sun melted into the sky leaving behind fading hues of red and gold

The sky would soon turn dark, and the evening would be cold

Tonight, however, my heart was overflowing with regret

There was someone I just couldn't forget

With every sunset was a day gone

A step away from you

I tried as hard as I could, but I couldn't banish you from my mind

I'd close my eyes and drift off to sleep and it's only your face I'd find

I'd see the stars twinkle in your eyes and the moon hide your gorgeous smile

I'd been looking for love in all the wrong places, when it was in front of me all the while

I just wish I'd seen earlier, how you filled the gaping hole in my heart

I wish I'd heard the truth in your words and felt the comfort of your embrace while I could

Because now it really hurts when we're so far apart...

How do I win your love once more, how do I mend what's broken?

I don't know what needs to be done, but my heart has already spoken

This distance between us, it is like an invisible wall

With me waiting on the other side, eager for your one call

Only it never comes, I never hear the innocence of your voice

But I will wait for you as I have no choice

Passion

You may not know it, but you're very special to me
And not because we're meant to be

But because you're my first love after all
And how can I part with my first love?

Passion

Senseless

You make me senseless
Everything about you
Even your smile makes my heart restless
With just one glance
You take away my calm demeanor
You make my heart leap and dance

You make me senseless
Perhaps it's the sound of your voice
That without it, I become restless
With just one look at your watch
You make me smile, that for the rest of the day
I miss your presence so much

You make me senseless
Even your silence reaches out to me
It makes me wonder; it makes me restless

Time and distance apart
You will always steal my heart
For its only you who can make me so restless
Only you who can leave me so breathless

Passion

The Princess

In the depths of the darkest hour
She waits in the tallest tower
While the rest of the world sleeps
Sometimes she smiles, sometimes she weeps

Trapped in a stone tower high above the sky
Allows not for her prince to come by
So, she waits, but does so restlessly
Resting her hands on the edge carelessly

She sighs and glares at the moon
Hoping that her prince will arrive soon
But dusk turns into dawn, the dark into light
And of her prince there is no sight

She turns away, her heart heavy with sadness
Building her walls this high was clearly madness
But if only they knew, it was the only way
Too many had left; all she had wanted was someone to stay

It was too late now she thought
How she had struggled and fought
But the walls were up and would stay so
They had begged but she said no

So, in her impenetrable castle she would stay
Waiting for her prince to sweep her away
Her fragile heart would stay under lock and key
For the one who was meant to be

Passion

In her yearning, he would surely arrive
To return passion once more to her life
He would surely answer her heart's call
She was a princess after all

Passion

The Silence of Love

They spoke neither
with words nor actions
Their love had
neither boundaries nor factions
Instead, it was their hearts
which spoke the most beautiful of words
Such sounds which put to shame
the voices of even the most melodious of birds

Such love that neither the sun
nor moon could come between
And in their glistening eyes could only
the flames of love be seen
If you watched from afar,
you would feel the eccentricity in the air
And you would see between two lovers,
such love that is rare

Time would indeed stop
and one could only watch
With enviousness,
of the love that no one could touch
Such love that smothered
even the darkest soul
And made what was once incomplete, whole

The kind of love that
made the heart leap
That ran true and deep
And that was forever to keep

Passion

Bound neither by promises nor yearning
Instead, it was the silence
that had the lover returning

The silence of love
That had neither speech nor sound
Instead by truth was it bound
Such love that each time you returned
Would only silence be found

Rescue Me

My eyes thirst for your sweet sight
And my arms yearn for your embrace
My mind wanders to you every night
And my heart searches only for your face

You have captured both the heart and soul
Lost I am in the allure of love that is so sweet
Now only you can dispel this fire and make me whole
I'll wait for you; I'll wait till we again meet

For I see something that no one else sees
In the depths of my heart your name is engraved
Love causes me pain but also my soul it frees
Hence is it only for you my heart I have saved

Every moment spent apart makes me restless
How I yearn to be captured in your arms
For you to kiss me again and leave me breathless
I wish to hear your voice as it soothes away my qualms

You have me trapped in your every memory
Your every word
I am the shadow to your every step
Your every movement

Indeed, you have tamed this wild heart
With the allure of love that never does cease
I wish for you to fill this blank space
Mend these distances so that we are not apart
Hold me close so that I may see those eyes tease

Passion

And smile flirtatiously and make my heart race

Rescue me,
From my own restlessness

Passion

Soul Deep

She stared long and deep into his eyes
Knowing that in their depths the truth lies
She saw longing mixed with desire
Felt the heat like a smoldering fire
They drew her in and held her, helpless
She saw kindness and a man who was selfless
He did not look away, and neither did she
His eyes mesmerized her and was all she could see

The world disappeared and time stood still
She drank in his soul but did not have her fill
It was not nearly enough, she wanted more
She wanted to dive deep, right into his core
She wanted to explore the maze of his mind
Wondering what buried emotions she would find
She wanted to read his every thought like a book
Wanting nothing more than to just look

She knew she had just scratched the surface
Beneath that, was more passion and more purpose
She was intrigued yet felt restless
His mere presence made her feel senseless
His eyes gave her a glimpse into his soul
Made her feel empty yet whole
The intensity burned her, but she could not resist
Her feelings of longing would not persist

His eyes were soul deep
So deep that it made her heart leap

Passion

A Little Bit of Magic

It all seems so surreal, like a dream come true
How is it so perfect? How is it we just knew?
There was no warning, just pure emotion
We moved like one, in synchronized motion

Like magic, like the moon and the stars
You showed me your world and I showed you my scars

From the ground you brought me up to the sky
Where castles we built and, on the clouds, I would lie
The walls that were once high tumbled to the ground
I looked down from my tower and my prince I found

Like magic, like the final piece of a puzzle
A perfect fit for you and me, a hidden escape to our castle

You showed me some of you and then more
Now I cannot help but search for you through every door
I look you for you in every crowd, in every place
For a familiarity, maybe your smile or a glimpse of your face
Like magic, like the symbol of yin and yang
Two opposites on the same side, whose fate in the universe does hang

All I know is that without a little bit of magic
Life would indeed be tragic

Passion

Heart Song

There was a quiet rhythm to her heartbeat, calm and steady
She kept the walls of her heart closed, always scared and never ready
Then she saw him, and was mesmerized, he was like none she had met
He was mysterious and so handsome, but still she was not sure yet

She drew herself into her castle, her safe space, keeping her heart reserved
He drew her out, or at least tried to, but she was not sure if her heart he deserved
Hours turned into days and days into months, as they spent more time together
She saw in him more of her than she realized, but could this really be forever?

Her walls slowly tumbled down, how could they not? He was so gentle and kind
He lit the fire of desire within her, captivated and enchanted her mind
Her heart jumped at the sound of his voice, her lips whispered his name
He did not know it, but her heart was his, but how could he ever feel the same?

He was incredible, strong, handsome, enchanting and she was shy and scared
It seemed careless to dive in so fast, but to him her soul she had bared
She gave every part of herself to him, heart, body, soul, to him she belonged
And when her world grew dark, there was only one person whose embrace she longed

Passion

Perhaps it was foolishness, or the allure of love, but how could she
walk away?

She knew there was no promise of forever, but he was the best part of
her day

So even if it hurt her, and it did, she would hold on, for he was worth
the pain

A thousand times over and a thousand more, she would do it all over
again

He was the song of her heart, the name on her lips and the light in
her eyes

Maybe he knew not, just how much he mattered, but the heart never
lies

Sometimes she got scared, that her love was too much, and it would
push him away

But in his arms, solace she would find, with a gentle touch he would
tell her it was all okay

And now finally her heart felt peace, for it had met him and known
love, so true and pure

No wrong he could do, would ever tarnish that, for if she was the
ailment, he was the cure

And if she walked away tomorrow, she would forever hold onto this
moment in time

Where she met a man so incredible and so selfless, he made her heart
sing and rhyme

Passion

Pain

Beautiful Nightmare

The fragrance of your soul touches me, just like every night
I toss and turn relentlessly, but it's a losing fight
Just like every night, you again steal my peace
Consuming my every thought, I see again those mischievous eyes
tease

I feel you in every heartbeat, I feel you in every being of my soul
Tonight, you've again come, tonight my sleep you've again stolen
But it doesn't matter, for I want nothing more than to be lost in your
arms
For you to hold me close and whisper in my ear, soothing away my
qualms

How I wish the night would never end
For in your arms, I want to forever spend
But you leave, and once again a cold empty place I find
A gaping hole, a lone tear... you've taken with you a piece of my mind

But you'll be back and waiting for me again tonight
For when my eyes I close, you will be the first sight
Under a starlit sky and a peeping moon
You will again return to me soon

Tonight, we shall again be one
One soul, one heartbeat
For in my scattered dreams, we shall again meet

Pain

Pained Release

The tears fell endlessly
Fat sparkling drops
I didn't dare stop them
It was to me a release
Of the pain
I so desperately tried to appease

Perhaps with every wound
There came a valuable lesson
Love just gets you ruined
I had an endless expectation
Perhaps too many a foolish dream
But now all that's left
Is complete devastation

I can feel the pain engulf me
It consumes me like a fire
Tearing through every memory
Of the love I will never see
The tears still fall
Like sparkling jewels
They leer at me

I want so bad to forget
Forget the nightmare
That has me trapped
I want to wish we never met
I want to walk away
But then the memories come back
And it hurts all over again

Pain

Each cut deeper than the next
It tears away at my soul
Leaving me empty and broken
These tears are a release
A pained release
Of the love that never will be

Pain

Reflections

I can't help but look back
to the day we met
With that dazzling smile and intense stare
you had my heart set
It didn't take much time
before you became both my day and night
At the time all I ever wanted
was to be captured by your sweet sight

With you I was free
and never had to think twice
It is only now I realize
that foolish mistakes do come at a painful price
The charm and exuberant personality
was what you wanted me to see
If only I had looked a little closer
I would have seen the love that never was to be

But alas, my foolish and naïve heart
blocked my true perception
I failed to see that your words and actions
were just mere reflections
They were no less to the rippling
tides of a pond
It was only after the water stilled that it became
clear, ours were a broken bond

You left as if you never appeared,
as if you never touched my soul
And so now I sit and wait for love

Pain

that will again make me whole
Never again will I be foolish to trust in love,
for I have lost all
My peace has been snatched
and loving you was my greatest downfall

You were after all never real
and neither was your love
They were both just reflections

Pain

Reminiscences

I will be leaving soon
No matter how much it pains me
Some things are just not meant to be
My heart is in ruin

I don't want to leave
But there is a path I must take
Away from you, is where myself I will make
My heart will grieve

Sometimes in life we have no choice
Just like I find myself now, helpless, and alone
Wasted time and spilled tears I have known
My heart will no longer leap to the sound of your voice

I wish to turn back the hands of time
Back when I was still held in your embrace
When I was still able to savor the details of your face
My heart will now lose its flame, its rhyme

I tried to make the most of the time remaining
Perhaps I didn't try hard enough
Or maybe I didn't allow myself to love
My heart will never stop its complaining

I know I won't be able to walk away
I did before and I regret it everyday
This time the heart has nothing to say
We will each have to carve our own way

Pain

I never liked goodbyes
They made me feel incomplete
But this time, I will have hope
That someday, we again will meet

Pain

Sweet Obsession

A blank page stares at me,
empty and cold
Just like your ice blue eyes,
one that stories it once behold
I hold onto my pen,
fingers poised
But words escape me,
my thoughts refusing to be voiced

It takes all my strength
not to rip the paper in pieces
But I crumple it anyway,
only to later smooth out the creases
I feel a void like no other,
one that threatens to tear me apart
An irresistible urge of sweet madness
that surges through my heart

But what can I do,
for your love has made me this way
How can I forget the empty promises
you made to me every single day
I had loved you
only to be cheated
I had tried to keep you by my side
only to be defeated

Where are the sweet dreams
you wove before me
The joy and happiness

Pain

you said would be
Were they too
an illusion you painted
To fool me so that I would
never see that your love was tainted

Your love may have brought me to my knees
It may have made me weak
And your betrayal may have silenced my heart
But now will only my hate speak
I am a lover wronged by love itself
And so will only love be my revenge
I won't stop loving you
Till my heartache I avenge

From now and till the end of time
Until you have paid for your crime
You will be my sweet obsession

Pain

Timeless Indulgences

I closed my weary eyes
I promised I would not ever
Not after all the countless lies
I knew what would happen
Once I slipped away
I would be lost in your memories
For the rest of the day

There would certainly be no returning
But I could not ignore that I too was hurting
Maybe this was my own way
Of dealing with the grief
Or perhaps my punishment for not
Stopping you as you tried to leave

It was a bitter pill to swallow
But the truth is that your memories
Had indeed left my heart hollow
If it means closing my eyes
To find you again
I'd do it not just once, not even twice
But a million times, for the truth is that
I find escape from the pain

Some call it self-destruction
But they know not the monsters I face
Drowning myself in your memories
Takes me to a better place
I find the peace I so greedily seek

Pain

Indulgences may be for the weak
But am I not?

This timeless solace sets me free
It is my only indulgence
My timeless indulgence

Pain

Winter's Wrath

Like an angel she descended,
smothered in folds of white
Casting her wand,
she ordered the cold wind to bite
Leaving in her wake
a trail of billowy white foam
She blew wisps of icy frost
commanding everyone to rush home

She ran wildly with the wind
and fought furiously with the snow
She cast clouds over the somber sky
while commanding the wind to blow
She spared nothing, not even the trees
for they all stood naked and bare
Swishing her wand from left to right
she commanded without a care

Her eyes blazed as she called
upon the storm, hushing the breeze
Lightning struck and thunder roared
indicating that her wrath was not to cease
Glittering jewels fell from the sky
on pavements slick with sleet
She stood in the midst like a goddess
satisfied that her work was now complete

This was the way of nature
as civilization soon would learn
As to cast away the shadows of autumn

Pain

she would have to again next year return
Though long it may take
she would be ready when the time came
It was her moment to shine and steal the sunlight
For winter was to always remain the same

Pain

Power

Lightness and Darkness

She loved the light
and how it made her feel
Those beautiful sunrises
and how her heart it would steal
Perfect white clouds
against a sea of bright blue
Just a whisper of a soft breeze
And colors of every hue

Sun dappled trees
with leaves gently swaying
The smell of spring in the air
and parks filled with kids playing
Yes, she loved the light
Everything beautiful and bright
But she craved the dark
Everything grey and stark

Charcoal colored skies
with twinkling stars
The song from the fireflies
and whispers of the wind
Embers of red
from the smoldering fire
The ground as a bed
laying under a starry canopy

Long nights
filled with restlessness
A dark abyss with no lights

Power

guided by the jewels in the sky
The light appeased her
But the dark drew her
The light healed her
But the dark sated her

Power

Savior

When the world felt dark, and I needed light
You were there by my side, day, and night
When I became afraid and would cry
You would reassure me and not lie
When I looked for comfort and found none
All I did was say I needed you and you were the one
When I fell into a pit of despair, you never lost hope
You gave me something to hold onto so I could cope

You held me up while felt apart, through each day
When I felt lost you knew just what to say
You never left me alone, you were always there
Though you could not hold me, you showed you care
You saved me every single time, you are my savior
Though you may disagree, it is to you I owe all favor

You were the rainbow after the storm
My blanket of hope to keep me warm
You were the beacon of light on a dark night
My glimmer of hope and such a beautiful sight
My savior, yes you. How do I show you?
I have so much to say but words a few
How do I thank you? How do I even start?
All I know is that you touched my soul and my heart

Power

Goddess

She rose from the ground up, like a tall, beautiful flower
They knew not of her gift to turn pain into power
She hid herself away, showing them only what they wanted
If she revealed too much, she would become the hunted

She was to them no threat, only beautiful and helpless
They came with their selfish wants, thinking that she was selfless
But they were wrong, they knew not of the power she kept
She treated them well still, even though many of them left

But they returned, they always did, how could they not?
They needed what she offered, not just a little but a lot
And she would give, she allowed them to drink from her soul
They had their fill, and while she became empty, they became whole

But still it was not enough, they wanted the power she wielded
They tried to take it from her, but in the end, it was them who
kneeled
She made them pay for all they took, made them shiver and quiver
They pleaded and begged, but still their blood ran like a river

And when all was done, she returned to her palace where she waited
For the one who was selfless and pure, for him she was created
He would seek not her power nor her beauty, instead he would offer
his soul
And after all the pain she would find peace again, for he would make
her whole

She was a goddess, a queen, she belonged on the throne
And when he came, on that day, she would no longer be alone
But wait she must, for all that took time was worth the wait
And so just this once, she left it all up to fate

Power

www.ingramcontent.com/pod-product-compliance
Lightning Source LLC
Chambersburg PA
CBHW060545030426
42337CB00021B/4446